DUE DATE

		AUG 28	1991
	MAR 20 1992	DEC 0 4 2002	
	MAY 1 6 1992	NOV 1 1 2006	
	JUL 2 2 1996		
	AUG 1 9 1996		
	NOV 1 6 2000		
	201-6503		Printed in USA

CANOEING

Norman Barrett

Franklin Watts

London   New York   Sydney   Toronto

First Paperback Edition 1990
ISBN 0-531-15178-6

© 1987 Franklin Watts

First published in Great Britain
    1987 by
Franklin Watts
12a Golden Square
London W1R 4BA

First published in the USA by
Franklin Watts Inc
387 Park Avenue South
New York
N.Y. 10016

First published in Australia by
Franklin Watts
14 Mars Road
Lane Cove
2066 NSW

UK ISBN: 0 86313 516 1
US ISBN: 0–531–10349–8
Library of Congress Catalog Card
Number 86–51222

Printed in Italy

Designed by
Barrett & Willard

Photographs by
All-Sport
All-Sport/Vandystadt
N.S. Barrett Collection
British Canoe Union

Illustrations by
Rhoda & Robert Burns

Technical Consultant
Geoff Good, Chief Coach British
    Canoe Union

Contents

Introduction

Canoeing is both a sport and a popular leisure activity. Canoeists enjoy paddling on rivers, canals and lakes and in the sea. Touring by canoe is an excellent way to explore inland or coastal regions.

Racing on rough water on special courses is one of the most exciting canoe sports. Canoe racing on calm water is an Olympic sport.

△ A competitor in a whitewater event battles to keep her kayak on course. Whitewater racing is held on special river courses, with fast-flowing water and hazards such as weirs and rocks.

There are two main types of canoes, the kayak and the Canadian canoe.

The canoeist sits inside the kayak, with legs outstretched under the deck. The kayak paddle has a blade at each end.

The Canadian canoe is usually open, although a spraydeck may be fitted. The canoeist sits or kneels, and uses a paddle with one blade.

△ "Fun" slalom events may be held in swimming pools. The canoeist here is taking part in a youth competition. This is a good way to learn how to control a canoe and maneuver it at speed before trying it on rough water.

The kayak and canoe

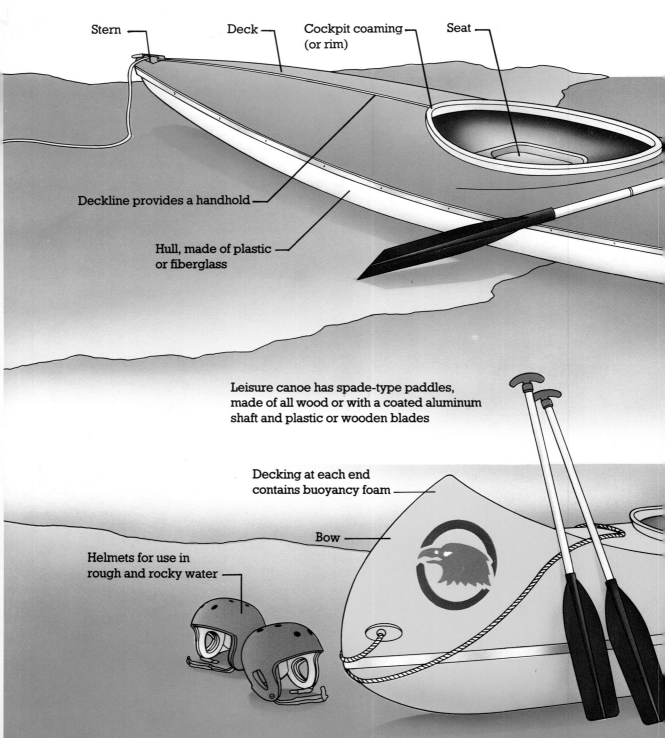

Stern

Deck

Cockpit coaming
(or rim)

Seat

Deckline provides a handhold

Hull, made of plastic
or fiberglass

Leisure canoe has spade-type paddles,
made of all wood or with a coated aluminum
shaft and plastic or wooden blades

Decking at each end
contains buoyancy foam

Bow

Helmets for use in
rough and rocky water

Touring kayak has double-ended paddle with blades
normally at 90 degrees to each other

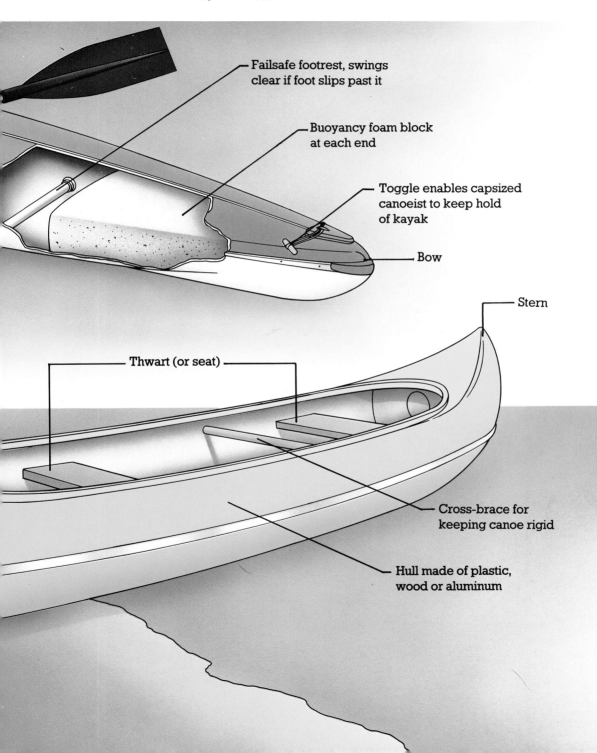

Failsafe footrest, swings
clear if foot slips past it

Buoyancy foam block
at each end

Toggle enables capsized
canoeist to keep hold
of kayak

Bow

Stern

Thwart (or seat)

Cross-brace for
keeping canoe rigid

Hull made of plastic,
wood or aluminum

Canoeing for fun

Canoeing may be enjoyed alone, but is best practiced in groups to start with. Beginners should learn in calm water, preferably under the supervision of a qualified person.

The beginner must be able to swim and should wear a life preserver. In addition to the paddling strokes, a beginner must learn how to carry the canoe and get in and out of it safely.

△ Paddling through some rough water in an open touring canoe. Life preservers are an important part of a canoeist's equipment. Light footwear should be used, because you cannot swim in heavy footwear.

Even experienced canoeists should never go out alone without telling someone of their plans. They should also find out about local conditions such as current or tides.

Other safety precautions include not overloading a canoe or changing places, and keeping clear of other craft and of hazards.

▽ Canoeists explore a rocky ravine in single kayaks. It is safer to tour in groups, and it is always a good plan to let someone know where you are going and about how long you expect to be.

△ One of the basic skills of sea canoeing is the paddle brace. The paddler leans toward a wave about to break and places the blade face down over the top of the wave. Leaning away from a wave is likely to cause a capsize.

◁ The pop up, one of the advanced skills practiced by surf canoeists.

▷ Shooting weirs like this is not for the beginner!

Canoe racing

There are several kinds of canoe racing, from 547 yd (500 m) sprints to marathons of up to 125 miles (200 km). Sprint racing takes place on calm water. Marathon courses usually include natural rivers.

A singles kayak is known as a K1, a doubles as a K2, and so on. Canadian canoes are known as C1, C2 and so on.

▷ The start of a K2 race in the Olympic Games. Sprints are held in lanes. There have been canoeing events in the Olympics since 1936.

▽ Spectators watch two canoeists racing neck and neck in a C1 event. In Canadian canoes, the competitors paddle in a high-kneeling position.

△ Officials make sure the canoes are level before the start of a race.

◁ In longer races, such as the 6.2 miles (10,000 m), there are no lanes. The canoeists race up and down a course, rounding a buoy at each end.

Sprints over 547 yd and 1,094 yd (500 and 1,000 m) are run in lanes. In major events, there are heats, the first three going through to the next round. The losers in the first round take part in a *repêchage*, or rerun, for a place in the next round.

The water on a sprint course must be as still as possible. Some courses have windbreaks to restrict the effect of cross-winds.

▽ A women's K4 at practice. There have been kayak events for women since the 1948 Olympics, but the K4 was a new event in 1984.

Marathon races are held on rivers, over distances of 3 miles (5 km) or more. In some long-distance races, more than 200 competitors take part.

The longest nonstop canoe race in the world is the international Devizes-to-Westminster race. It is held every year in southern England, over 125 miles (200 km) of canals and rivers.

△ With night falling, competitors in the annual Devizes-to-Westminster race are still paddling hard. Senior crews have completed the course in under 16 hours. Junior crews and singles classes are allowed three overnight stops.

Portage

In marathon racing or touring on rivers and canals, difficult obstacles such as rapids and waterfalls have to be negotiated. This may be done by portage—carrying the kayak or canoe around obstacles, including dams.

In a marathon that has several portages, the speed of portaging is important.

▽ Most portages are easier than this, and simply mean carrying the canoe along the river bank. But mountain expeditions might involve climbing down steep rocky slopes.

Whitewater racing

Whitewater racing takes place on rough water. There are two main types of competition, slalom and wildwater racing. The competitors cross the starting line at intervals.

In slalom racing, the canoeists have to negotiate a number of "gates" on a winding course.

In wildwater racing, competitors are timed over a course of 3 miles (5 km) or more.

△ Uneven and rocky, a slalom course is a severe test of a canoeist's skill and control. The gates are pairs of poles hanging over the water. There are usually 25 to 30 gates on a course. Some have to be paddled through upstream and some downstream. Time penalties are added to a canoeist's time for touching (5 sec) or missing (50 sec) gates.

It is easy to see from these slalom pictures how the term whitewater first came to be used.

Kayak singles and Canadian singles and pairs take part. Both kayaks and canoes are fitted with watertight spraydecks.

▷ A wildwater course has at least 2 miles (3 km) of rough, fast-flowing water, with rapids, rocks and other obstacles.

Competitors start out at intervals, and the aim is to complete the course in as fast a time as possible.

The art of wildwater racing is to be able to "read" the course, to find the fastest route through the rapids. Experienced canoeists can tell which route to take by the pattern of the currents and the shape of the surface waves.

Other canoe activities

◁ Outrigger canoeing is a traditional sport in the Pacific Ocean, especially in Hawaii. An outrigger extends from the side of the canoe with a buoy to steady the boat.

▽ River rafting is a popular touring activity in some countries. The craft is an unsinkable rubber raft that carries six to nine people.

▷ Canoe polo is played between teams of five. The object of the game is to score goals by throwing the ball to hit a 3.3 ft (1 m) square board standing 6 ft (2 m) above the water.

▽ The paddles may be used to stop the ball in the air or to draw it over the water, but not to hit it. The player with the ball may be "tackled."

Touring by canoe is becoming an increasingly popular activity. The pictures on these pages show touring on different kinds of water, from placid streams to turbulent rapids.

As a canoeist becomes more skilled and experienced, he or she can tackle more difficult waters. Provided the safety rules are always followed, canoe touring is a fine outdoor activity for people of all ages.

The story of canoeing

The first canoes

Canoes were among the first means of transport. Craft similar to canoes were used by people 6,000 years ago. Modern canoes were developed from those used by the American Indians and Eskimos.

△ A first lesson in canoeing for an Eskimo, from a drawing made over a hundred years ago.

The Canadian canoe

In the forests, people hollowed out logs to make "dugout" canoes, for use on rivers and lakes. As people became more skilled, they built canoes with planks or wooden frames covered with bark.

These simple craft were developed by the North American Indians. They stretched buffalo skins over a wooden framework to make an open boat. The canoeist knelt on one knee and used a single-bladed paddle. This style of boat became known as the Canadian canoe.

△ A Canadian canoe in a North American forest in pioneering days.

The Eskimo kayak

The only wood available to the Eskimos of the Arctic lands was driftwood found floating in the icy seas. But they had skins and bones from seals and whales. They stretched skins over a framework of driftwood or bone to make their kayaks.

△ John MacGregor in the first Rob Roy canoe. It could be sailed as well as paddled.

Pleasure and competition

It was not until 1865 that canoes first began to be used chiefly for pleasure. A Scottish canoeist and traveller, John MacGregor, designed a canoe that could be both paddled and sailed. It was called the "Rob Roy."

In 1866, the Royal Canoe Club was formed at Twickenham, in England, and a year later a regatta was held for Rob Roy canoes. But canoeing activity wasn't really popular until folding canoes were introduced in the early 1900s. These could be more easily transported.

Major events

Canoeing was first included in the Olympics in 1936 in the form of racing over 1,094 yd (1,000 m) and 10,936 yd (10,000 m). There were events for kayaks, folding kayaks and Canadian canoes.

Slalom racing was started in the mountains of Austria and Germany in the 1930s. The first world championships were held in Geneva, Switzerland, in 1949. Wildwater racing first appeared in the world championships in 1959. But whitewater events have been included only once in the Olympics, in 1972, when slalom races were held.

Touring

Canoeing has grown as a pastime, too. Most countries have canoeing clubs, where enthusiasts get together to paddle on rivers and lakes or along coastlines. Many people take canoeing vacations, touring and exploring regions of beauty and interest on the waterways of the world.

△ The Swedish pair who won a gold medal in the 1936 Olympics in the 10,000 m event for folding kayaks.

△ A canoe expedition along the Grand Canyon. Not all parts of the Colorado River are so placid.

Facts and records

Most golds

The canoeist with the most Olympic gold medals is a Swedish kayak racer, Gert Fredrickson, with six. He won the 1,000 m title at three consecutive Games (1948 to 1956), two 10,000 m titles (1948 and 1956) and the 1,000 m pairs in 1960.

The Soviet canoeist Vladimir Parfenovich won a record three golds in one Olympics (1980), the 500 m kayak singles and the 500 m and 1,000 m kayak pairs.

△ The record-breaking Gert Fredrickson of Sweden.

Seven-up

The biggest international racing canoe was the seven-man Canadian canoe, measuring 36 ft (11 m) from bow to stern, which raced over 547 yd (500 m). The canoeists paddled on alternate sides, with the back man responsible for steering. The event has now been dropped from championship racing and replaced by the C4.

△ A seven-man Canadian canoe.

The water quintain

Perhaps the earliest recorded instance of canoes being used in sport was the water quintain. This was a popular pastime on the River Thames in London over 700 years ago. A canoe was paddled furiously toward a pole fixed in the river. A young man with a lance, standing in the canoe, aimed to strike a shield or board on top of the pole and break the lance against it. If he failed to break the lance, he was sure to be thrown into the water.

△ The water quintain.

Glossary

Bow
The front of a canoe

Canadian canoe
A canoe propelled with a single-bladed paddle, usually from a kneeling position.

Capsize
To overturn the canoe.

Coaming
Rim of cockpit on a kayak.

Deck
Top surface of canoe or kayak.

Gate
Pair of poles on slalom course.

Hull
The body of the canoe.

Kayak
Enclosed canoe paddled in a sitting position with a double-bladed paddle.

Life preserver
A sleeveless jacket worn to help a capsized canoeist stay afloat.

Lock
An enclosure for raising or lowering boats at a place where the water level changes.

Outrigger
A float on the end of a beam extending from the side of a canoe.

Portage
Carrying the canoe around an obstruction.

Repêchage
In racing, a rerun to give losers another chance.

Slalom
Racing through a series of gates on rough water.

Spraydeck
Skirt that fits around paddler's waist and attaches to coaming, to stop water getting into the canoe.

Stern
Back end of the canoe.

Weir
Dam that controls the level of the river.

Whitewater
Any water where the turbulence creates foam, giving it a white appearance.

Index